DECLARATION

•

I hereby declare that
all the paper produced
by Cartiere del Garda S.p.A.
in its Riva del Garda mill
is manufactured completely
<u>Acid-free and Wood-free</u>

Dr. Alois Lueftinger
Managing Director and General Manager
Cartiere del Garda S.p.A.

GREEN WORLD

CACTI
AND OTHER SUCCULENTS

Written by
Wendy Madgwick

STECK-VAUGHN
LIBRARY
A Division of Steck-Vaughn Company

Austin, Texas

Editors: Amanda Wood, Wendy Madgwick
Designer: Jane Hunt
Illustrator: Sallie Reason
Consultant: Nigel Taylor

Notes to Reader
There are some words in this book that are printed in **bold** type.
A brief explanation of these words is given in the glossary on p. 44.

All living things are given two Latin names when first classified by a
scientist. Some of them also have a common name, for example, giant
saguaro, *Carnegiea gigantea*. In this book, the common name is used where
possible, but the scientific name is given when first mentioned.

Library of Congress Cataloging-in-Publication Data

Madgwick, Wendy, 1946-
Cacti : and other succulents / written by Wendy Madgwick.
p. cm. – (The Green world)
Includes index.
Summary: Describes the many varieties of cacti and other succulent
plants found around the world.
ISBN 0-8114-2737-4
1. Cactus – Juvenile literature. 2. Succulent plants – Juvenile literature.
[1. Cactus. 2. Succulent plants.] I. Title. II. Series.
QK495.C11M23 1991
583'.47 – dc20   91-14934
CIP   AC

Color separations by Chroma Graphics, Singapore
Printed and bound by L.E.G.O., Vicenza, Italy
1 2 3 4 5 6 7 8 9 0 LE 96 95 94 93 92

Photographic credits
t = top, b = bottom, l = left, r = right
Cover: Bruce Coleman; page 9 N.P. Taylor; page 10 Frank Lane/
K.G. Preston-Mafham; page 13 N.P. Taylor; page 17 Bruce Coleman/
A. Compost; page 19 Bruce Coleman/Duscher; page 20 N.P. Taylor;
page 22 Bruce Coleman/J. Shaw; page 24 Frank Lane/Eric and David
Hosking; page 25 Harry Smith Collection; page 26 Smith/Polunin
Collection; page 29*t* Bruce Coleman/D.B. Bartlett; page 29*b* Frank
Lane/K.G. Preston-Mafham; page 30 Frank Lane/K. G. Preston Mafham;
page 31*t* Harry Smith Collection; page 31*b* N.P. Taylor; page 35
Bruce Coleman/J. & D. Bartlett; page 36 Frank Lane/Prema Photos;
page 37 Bruce Coleman/Charlie Ott; page 40 Frank Lane Picture Agency;
page 41 The Mansell Collection.

CONTENTS

GREEN WORLD

This tree shows the different groups of plants that are found in the world. It does not show how they developed or their relationship with each other.

MONOCOTYLEDONS

- One seed-leaf
- Leaves have parallel veins

Agave family (Agavaceae)
- Leaf succulents often forming a rosette

Aloe family (Aloeaceae)
- Leaf succulents
- Aloe, Haworthia, and Gasteria from Africa

DICOTYLEDONS

- Two seed-leaves
- Leaves have network of veins

Cactus family (Cactaceae)
- Stem succulents
- Spines and flowers grow from areoles
- Fruit or seed pod is a berry

Mesembryanthemum family (Aizoaceae)
- Leaf succulents from Africa

Portulaca family (Portulacaceae)
- Mostly leaf and root succulents from the Americas, Africa, and Australia

Asclepiad family (Asclepiadaceae)
- Leaf, stem, and root succulents from Africa, Australia, and Asia

Euphorbia family (Euphorbiaceae)
- Stem and root succulents
- Spurges of Africa and America

Crassula family (Crassulaceae)
- Stem, leaf, and root succulents
- Often form rosette shapes

CONIFEROUS (OR FIR) TREES (Gymnosperms)

FLOWERING PLANTS (Angiosperms)

FERNS, CLUB MOSSES, AND HORSETAILS (Pteridophytes)

MOSSES AND LIVERWORTS (Bryophytes)

ALGAE

GREEN PLANTS

PLANTS

ANIMALS

FUNGI AND LICHENS

BACTERIA

SLIME MOLDS

LIVING THINGS

The land area of the world is divided into ten main zones depending on the plants that grow there. Succulents are found throughout the world in areas that usually lack water.

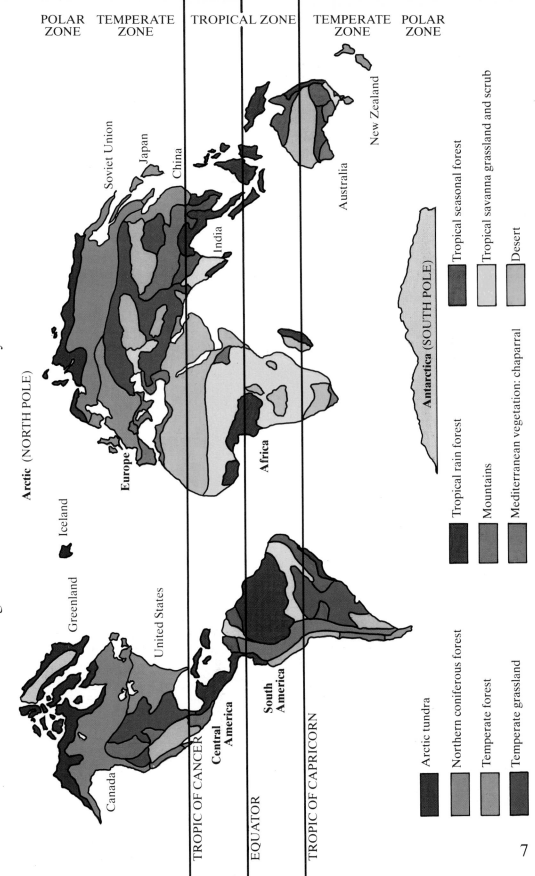

POLAR ZONE   TEMPERATE ZONE   TROPICAL ZONE   TEMPERATE ZONE   POLAR ZONE

Soviet Union
Japan
China
India
Europe
Africa
Iceland
Greenland
United States
Canada
Central America
South America
Arctic (NORTH POLE)
New Zealand
Australia
Antarctica (SOUTH POLE)

TROPIC OF CANCER
EQUATOR
TROPIC OF CAPRICORN

Arctic tundra
Northern coniferous forest
Temperate forest
Temperate grassland

Tropical rain forest
Mountains
Mediterranean vegetation: chaparral

Tropical seasonal forest
Tropical savanna grassland and scrub
Desert

7

SUCCULENTS

Succulent plants, including cacti, come in all shapes and sizes but they all have one thing in common – they can store water. They are true **xerophytes**, able to withstand periods of prolonged drought. Their ability to survive in difficult conditions, including large changes in temperature from over 100°F at midday to below freezing at night, has allowed them to **colonize** many different **habitats** in every region of the world.

Succulents are a collection of unrelated plants found in over 500 groups or genera, 93 of which are in the cactus family. Most succulents belong to plant families in the major group known as **angiosperms**, or flowering plants (see p. 6 and p. 28). They are often grouped together according to whether they store water in the stem, the leaves, or the roots. Cacti and euphorbias are typical stem succulents. Crassulas and mesembryanthemums are juicy leaf succulents. Root succulents, in which the swollen roots or stem base often form a fleshy **caudex**, come from many plant families, including passion flowers, euphorbias, cucumbers, and convolvulus.

All over the world

Most people think of succulents, particularly cacti, as plants of hot deserts. This is true of some, but they are also found high up on cold, rocky mountains, in semi-arid savanna (grasslands), in cold, often icy, deserts, and in tropical forests. Their curious shapes and patterns of growth reflect the harsh conditions in which they live.

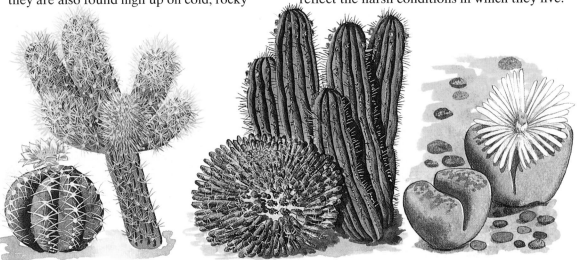

Cacti are found throughout the Americas, and take many forms.

Some African euphorbias are stem succulents and look like cacti. Others are root succulents.

African mesembryanthemums, leaf succulents, take many forms.

Origins?

Succulent plants probably **evolved**, or slowly changed, from normal leafy plants as the conditions in their habitats became drier. Not all the members of a plant family need necessarily be succulents; not even all cacti are succulents. For example, *Pereskia* (shown right), has a normal leafy form and grows and flowers like a wild rose. Some cactus seedlings produce fully developed leaves like ordinary plants; these are lost as they mature. It may be that *Pereskia* is very similar to the plants that gave rise to other modern-day cacti.

■ Succulents are green plants that make their own food by the process of **photosynthesis** (see p. 21).
■ They store water in their leaves, stems, or roots and can withstand periods of drought.
■ Most of them are angiosperms or flowering plants.
■ Most are **dicotyledons** (two seed-leaves). A few are **monocotyledons** (one seed-leaf).

African aloes (the aloe family) come in all shapes and sizes, from tiny clumps to giant trees.

The crassula family, for example sedums, grow in Europe, Africa, the Americas, and the East, often on mountain slopes.

The thick, stiff leaves of agaves from the southern U.S. and Mexico often form rosettes.

The Australian and Asian hoyas are climbers with thick, fleshy leaves.

NORTH AMERICA

North America is home to many succulents, especially cacti, which, with one exception, are native only to the Americas. Cacti differ from other succulents because they bear tiny cushionlike growing points called **areoles**, from which their spines and flowers develop. Their green, fleshy stems are often ribbed or covered with **tubercles** (flat or raised growths) to allow them to swell with water.

The stem is also green because it contains the pigment **chlorophyll** which is used for photosynthesis (see p. 21). The spines, which range from fine, downy hairs to large, tough spikes, cut down water loss and may help to protect the plants against browsing animals.

The spread of particular kinds of cacti varies enormously. Some cacti such as *Opuntia* and *Escobaria* grow as far north as southern Canada; others are found only in the southern states of the U.S. The desert regions in particular are renowned for the variety and splendor of their cacti.

Apart from cacti, other stem succulents such as agaves are native to the U.S. Leaf succulents such as echeverias and sedums, and root and leaf succulents like *Lewisia* are also common.

Sonoran Desert
In the Sonoran Desert of Arizona and Mexico, spiny *Opuntia* cacti such as teddy bear cholla and organ pipe cacti often grow in dense clusters.

- ■ Cacti are dicotyledons with thick, fleshy stems.
- ■ The leaves are reduced to spines borne on areoles.
- ■ Photosynthesis takes place in the stem (see p. 21).
- ■ The **stomata** (small holes) are few and often sunken (see p. 21).

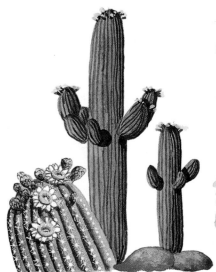

Ferocactus species

These are ribbed, globular cacti with long, fierce spines. They vary in height from a few inches to over 10 feet. *F. emoryi* (above) from Arizona and Mexico grows up to 10 feet tall.

Carnegiea gigantea

The giant saguaro cactus is native to Arizona and northwest Mexico. Large specimens, hundreds of years old, can grow to over 50 feet high and weigh up to 6 tons.

Lewisia species

These are mostly low-growing root succulents. The leaves, which may also be fleshy, form a rosette. The flowers are borne on long stems. *L. rediviva* (bitterroot, above) has a fleshy root that is said to be edible.

Escobaria species

These are mostly small cacti with round, spiny green stems with tubercles, and trumpet-shaped flowers. *E. vivipara* (above) grows in southern Canada and the U.S.

Echinocereus species

These can be round, cylindrical, spreading, clustered or solitary cacti. The stems are usually spiny and ridged with distinct ribs. Flowers are often large and beautiful. *E. viridiflorus* (above) is a native of the southern states.

Dudleya species

These leaf succulents belong to the crassula family. Their leaves all form rosettes with a layer of dead leaves at the base. *D. farinosa* (above) from California has clusters of pale yellow flowers.

CENTRAL & SOUTH AMERICA

Cacti and other succulents are widespread throughout Central and South America from Mexico to the tip of southern Argentina. Mexico, the so-called "home" of the cactus, has by far the most native species. They vary from tiny, low-growing forms to the large organ-pipes that tower high above the desert. Farther south, cacti such as *Peniocereus*, *Ferocactus*, and *Opuntia* abound. Even in the near freezing, arid mountains, many cacti, agaves, and yuccas survive.

Some cacti like *Schlumbergera* and *Rhipsalis* are **epiphytes**. They have flattened, leaflike stems and grow in the rain forests of Brazil and Central America. Recently, new species of cacti have been discovered on the barren Andean mountains of Peru. Succulents flourish in northern Chile, even in the coastal deserts where fog is the only source of moisture. Succulents grow in Bolivia, Paraguay, and Argentina, even along the snow line, while Patagonia is home to a few unusual cacti as well as puyas.

Mammillaria species
Mammillaria is a large group of small, round cacti with many hairy or prickly spines. Flowers often grow in a circle. They are found in the U.S., Mexico, and Central America. *M. senilis* (above) grows 8,800 feet up in the Mexican mountains.

Echeveria species
Echeverias are found throughout the Americas, some in cold mountain regions. The fleshy leaves often form dense clusters or rosettes that may help to trap heat. They are often smooth with small pronounced tips, as in *E. agavoides* (above).

Rhipsalis species
These are mostly epiphytes from the rain forests of Central and South America, especially southeast Brazil. The stems are cylindrical or flattened and may be leaflike and ribbed. Flowers often grow along the length of the stem, as in *R. russellii* (above) from Brazil.

Mexican cacti
Globose cacti such as
Echinocactus platyacanthus
(see left) and the tall, white-
haired "old man of the desert"
(*Cephalocereus senilis*) typify
the desert landscapes of
Mexico.

Maihuenia species
These are mostly small, shrubby
cacti from southern Chile and
Argentina. *M. poeppigii*
(above) has branching,
rounded stems that bear a
spike of green leaves at the tip.
The flowers are yellow and
funnel-shaped.

Agave species
Agaves form rosettes that vary
in size from dwarves to giants.
A. americana (above), the
century plant of Mexico, has
thick, spiny-edged leaves up to
6 feet long. When the plants
flower, the main rosette of
leaves dies.

Cereus species
Cereus are all tall, stately,
many-branched cacti from
South America. The stems are
ribbed, with long, dark spines.
They have large white flowers
that open at night and juicy red
fruits. *C. chalybaeus* (above)
grows in Argentina.

AFRICA

The African continent, with its vast areas of desert, semiarid savanna grasslands, rain forests, humid mountain slopes and steep valleys, is host to a multitude of succulents. There is only one native species of cactus (*Rhipsalis baccifera*). However, an amazing display of aloes, euphorbias, mesembryanthemums, stapelias, and other succulents, often looking like cacti, color the landscape.

There are many unusual forms, such as the baobab tree (*Adansonia digitata*) with its wrinkled, swollen trunk. Another, the cone-bearing *Welwitschia*, is a **gymnosperm** from the Namibian desert. Its long, wind-torn leaves straggle over the sands, soaking up the dew into their spongy tissues. Off the African coast, the island of Madagascar has its own unusual species, such as *Pachypodium,* which can reach treelike proportions.

Many forms

Members of the mesembryanthemum family are found throughout Africa. They come in many different shapes and sizes.

Lithops or living stones are reduced to two succulent leaves.

Carpobrotus has branched stems with thick, fleshy leaves.

Conophytum are dwarf plants with two united leaves.

Ruschia are shrubby and the branches are covered with the remains of dead leaves.

Faucaria are compact plants with "toothed" leaves.

Nananthus have swollen tuberous roots and tufts of leaves.

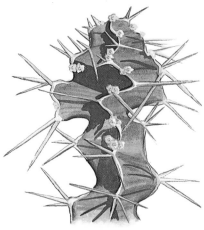

Pachypodium species

These are shrubby plants with a fleshy trunk or caudex. They vary in height from about 4 inches to over 30 feet (*P. geayi*, above). The leaves are often leathery and hairy and are borne in a cluster at the end of the stem.

Euphorbia species

Euphorbias, or spurges, are found in many areas. All species have a milky **sap** which can be poisonous and must never be allowed to get into the eyes. Many are very thorny (*E. grandicornis*, above), but a few are thornless.

Trichocaulon species

Trichocaulon have thick, fleshy, round or cylindrical stems covered with dense tubercles. Many have bristles at the tip. The flowers are often lobed and are borne right at the tip of the stem (*T. cactiforme*, above).

Kalanchoe species

Kalanchoe grow in tropical and subtropical areas. Leaf succulents, they can be bushy or climbing plants with large flat leaves with serrated edges or small smooth leaves. Some, like *K. tomentosa* (above), have a felty covering of hairs.

Stapelia species

Stapelias all have fleshy stems, often bearing fine hairs. Most of them have large star-shaped flowers, up to 14 inches in diameter in *S. gigantea* (above). The flowers smell of rotting meat and attract flies for pollination.

Aloe species

Aloes are very distinctive leaf succulents with striking flowers. They vary from dwarf rosettes to giant "trees." The leaves are usually long and narrow, tapering at the end. Many are stiff with toothed edges, as in *A. arborescens* (above).

15

AUSTRALIA AND ASIA

The continent of Australia has a few extraordinary succulents. They range from tiny plants such as *Portulaca* and *Calandrinia* to the tropical climbing *Hoya* and the swollen-trunked bottle or elephant trees (*Brachychiton* and *Adansonia*).

Some of the most fascinating plants of this region are those that form associations with ants. For example, the epiphyte *Dischidia* has two types of leaves. One kind is small, round, and succulent; the other larger leaves form round or elongated "pitchers" that trap water.

The plant's roots grow into these pitchers. Ants often use them as shelters, and the rotting remains of plants collected by the ants provide the *Dischidia* with minerals and nutrients. Other "ant plants" native to this area are *Myrmecodia* and *Hydnophytum*. Their large, juicy roots contain a wealth of tunnels. Ants often make their nests there.

Many succulents found in Japan (*Meterostachys* and *Orostachys*) and China (*Rhodiola*, *Sinocrassula*, and *Sedum*) grow high in the mountains. They are often low-growing and can withstand ice and snow.

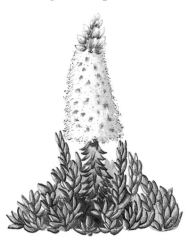

Orostachys species
In these dwarf plants the leaves form a fleshy rosette. They often have a bristle at the tip. The small flowers often form a dense flowerhead. *O. japonicus* (above) will grow in frost and snow.

Calandrinia species
These are a group of small or shrubby succulents native to south and west Australia. *C. polyandra* (above) has long, fleshy, spade-shaped leaves with masses of pink flowers which only open in the sun.

Sedum species
Sedums grow in many areas. The ice plant, *S. spectabile* (above), from China has fleshy roots, stems, and leaves. It can grow up to 10 inches, and has a flat flowerhead made of many star-shaped flowers.

Hoya species

Often called wax flowers, these are mainly succulent climbing plants. The leaves are thick and waxy to cut down water loss. The clusters of flowers are usually fragrant, as in *H. carnosa* (above).

Dischidia species

Most species are epiphytes with long, thin, trailing stems. *D. rafflesiana* (above) has small fleshy leaves and larger pitcher-shaped ones that trap water and are home to ants.

Portulaca species

Most are low-growing, spreading plants with succulent, almost cylindrical leaves. The small cup-shaped flowers open in the sun and close in the shade. *P. decipiens* (above) is found in several areas of Australia.

Ant plants

Myrmecodia species, like this one growing in Indonesia (see left), are succulent epiphytes that grow on the upper branches of tropical trees. Many are small shrublike plants with a large succulent caudex up to 6 inches in diameter. This is riddled with galleries that form nests for stinging ants. Some of the tunnels are used by the ants to store waste material, and this provides valuable nutrients and minerals that the plant absorbs.

17

EUROPE

Many of the succulents of Europe are found growing on stony mountainsides. They belong mostly to the crassula family and many form a typical rosette shape that allows the maximum surface for photosynthesis (see p. 21) in the minimum space. The leaves sometimes curl up in very dry weather to cut down on water loss due to **transpiration** (see p. 21).

Stonecrops (sedums) grow in rocky areas in Britain and farther south into the mountains of Spain and Portugal. *Sempervivum*, the houseleek, grows high in the southern Alps through to the Pyrenees and northwest Yugoslavia. Other succulent plants, such as *Caralluma*, flourish in Spain. The Canary Islands and Madeira are host to more spectacular flowering forms such as *Aeonium*, *Greenovia*, and *Aichryson*. Some of these can grow to over 3 feet in height, though most form low-growing rosettes. Many exotic cacti, agaves, and aloes have been introduced into the warm Mediterranean region and flourish there.

Sempervivum species
Most European species are low-growing plants with hairy leaves forming rosette-shaped cushions. These trap heat, helping the plant to withstand the cold mountain nights. The houseleek *S. hirtum* (above) is found in the Alps.

Aichryson species
Native to Madeira and the Canary Islands, *Aichryson* species are found mostly in mountain regions. They are low-growing plants with stems crowned by rosettes of hairy, spoon-shaped leaves like *A. dichotomum* (above).

Caralluma species
Many are creeping, often leafless, plants with fleshy stems. The stems are often branched and form trailing, cushionlike mats. The flowers are small, usually dark red or purple. *C. europaea* (above) grows in the Mediterranean.

Houseleeks

The houseleek family (*Sempervivum* species) is mostly European in origin. The cobweb houseleek (*S.arachnoideum*, shown left) grows in Switzerland. People used to plant houseleeks on the roofs of their houses. It was thought that they protected the house from being struck by lightning! They all have beautifully marked leaves that form a rosette. Houseleeks often grow close together in groups and many have spectacular flowers.

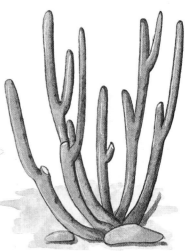

Aeonium species

The beautifully marked leaves form a tight rosette and the flower is borne on a long stem. Some like *A. arboreum* (above) grow to over 3 feet with a long spike of flowers. Others form low-growing rosettes with short hairy stems.

Sedum species

Stonecrops grow in mountains or dry, rocky areas. Those of Europe like *S. dasyphyllum* (above) usually form low-growing cushions made up of small globular-shaped leaves. The star-shaped flowers form a dense flowerhead.

Ceropegia species

Many are climbing plants; a few form shrubs. Some have swollen roots and juicy stems. The flowers often form lantern shapes. Many are native only to Asia and Africa, but *C. dichotoma* (above) grows in the Canaries.

STRUCTURE AND FORM

Most succulents are slow growing and their shape and form often reflect the way in which they live. For example, many cacti are small and globular, surviving either singly or in clusters. Their round shape means that little of their surface is exposed to the hot sun and drying winds. This keeps water loss and overheating to a minimum. A similar effect is achieved by some leaf succulents in which the hairy leaves form ground-hugging rosettes or spreading mats.

Column shapes are also very effective. At midday, when the sun is overhead and at its hottest, it only shines on the tops of these cacti. The rest of the plant is in the shade so water loss and overheating are reduced.

Columnar cacti are often large when mature, as are many African euphorbias. Some cacti can collect and store several quarts of water in one day of rain. The water content may form up to 90 percent of the weight of the plant. Many such succulents have a woody framework that keeps the body of the plant from collapsing when the water reserves are used up and the storage tissue shrinks. Many can lose up to 30 percent of their water content without dying.

Desert monsters
Cacti come in all shapes and sizes. Some, like *Pachycereus pringlei* (shown above), grow to enormous heights. The person at the base of this cactus is about 5 feet 6 inches tall.

Green Stems

The leaves of many stem succulents are reduced, often to spines. The green stems have therefore taken over the jobs of photosynthesis, **respiration**, and transpiration.

In respiration, oxygen is used to break down food to release energy. Carbon dioxide is released. In photosynthesis, the green pigment chlorophyll uses the energy in sunlight to combine carbon dioxide with water and minerals to form starches, fats, and proteins. Oxygen is released. The food is carried around the plant in **phloem** vessels.

In transpiration, water is absorbed through the roots, carried round the plant in **xylem** vessels, and lost as water vapor through stomata in the leaf or stem. To reduce water loss, the stomata are widely spaced, sunk into pits, and often closed during the heat of the day. A thick, waxy skin and a fine covering of hairs also reduce water loss and protect the plant from the sun's rays.

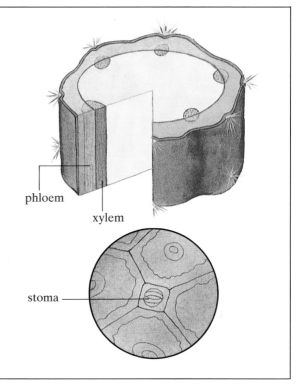

phloem

xylem

stoma

Shaped for survival

Some African euphorbias and American cacti look alike. Both groups have lost their leaves and developed a tough, juicy stem and a thick, slimy sap that absorbs water. This is an example of convergent evolution – where unrelated plants and animals in similar habitats develop in similar ways.

Many succulents have ridged stems. The stomata lie in the dip between the ridges so that they are not directly exposed to the sun and wind. Any moisture that is lost is trapped between the ridges. This also cuts down the rate of transpiration. Ridged stems also act like an accordion, swelling outward as the plant fills with water and folding inward as the water is used up.

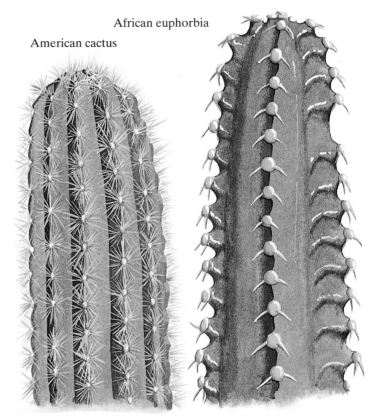

African euphorbia

American cactus

SPINES OR PADS?

The leaves of succulents come in as many shapes and sizes as the plants themselves. In cacti the leaves are reduced to spines or hairs. The stems have thick, waxy skins, or **cuticles**, and the stomata are widely spaced, keeping water loss to a minimum. For example, the water loss from *Opuntia* is less than 4 percent of that from an equal area of thin leaf. Such modifications allow them to live in the driest areas.

Leaf succulents generally grow in damper conditions – on mountains, in semidesert, and in salt marshes.

During dry weather, the leaves lose water and wrinkle up. When it rains, the plant takes up water and the leaves swell. As much as 90 percent of the leaf's weight may be stored water. The leaves have a thick, waxy cuticle and the stomata are often sunken in pits to reduce transpiration. Some leaves have a felty or woolly surface that cuts down on water loss and helps keep the leaf cool. In mountain plants a hairy surface can also insulate the plant against the cold, in addition to protecting it from the sun's harmful ultraviolet rays.

Storing carbon dioxide, saving water

In order for plants to live and grow, they have to respire and photosynthesize. To do so, the stomata have to be open to take in and release oxygen and carbon dioxide, but this may mean that too much water is lost. Some cacti and succulents have overcome this problem by collecting carbon dioxide during the night and storing it as an acid. This means that the stomata can be closed in the heat of the day and the plant can turn this stored acid into the sugars that it needs. Some succulents can also store the carbon dioxide produced during respiration by changing it into a chemical called malic acid.

Spines and glochids

All cactus spines, though they may vary greatly in size, are modified leaves. Fierce spines serve as protection against browsing animals. Hairs and prickles cut down on evaporation and trap dew, channeling the water down to the roots.

Fine, woolly hairs can protect against the cold of the night as well as the rays of the sun. The bristles, or glochids, of *Opuntia* are different. These bristles are barbed. If they penetrate the skin, they may break off and can be annoying. You should not touch them.

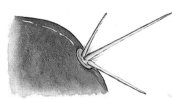

Opuntia species have sharp, detachable bristles.

Mammillaria hahniana has dense, hairlike bristles.

Turbinicarpus valdezianus has fine, comblike spines.

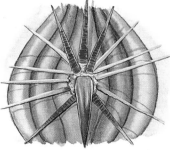

Ferocactus latispinus, the "devil's tongue," has large, hooked spines.

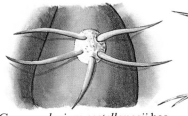

Gymnocalycium castellanosii has long spines radiating from a central point.

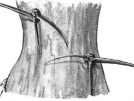

Cereus spegazzinii has single, thornlike spines.

Fleshy leaves

Succulent leaves often have thin-walled, elastic cells, which can shrink or swell with water. They can take many forms.

The fleshy leaves of *Echeveria agavoides* form a rosette.

The leaves of *Crassula barbata* are covered with long, fine hairs.

Cotyledon undulata has thick, wavy-edged leaves.

Sedum dasyphyllum forms dense rosettes that trap heat.

The cylindrical, pointed leaves of *Senecio haworthii* are coated with a white felt that protects them from the harsh rays of the sun.

Lithops salicola, stone plants, have two large fleshy leaves.

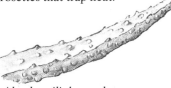

Aloe humilis leaves have tubercles, irregular white prickles and toothed margins.

ROOT SYSTEMS

Plant roots fulfill two functions: they take in water and anchor the plant in the soil. Some succulents have long tap roots; others have a vast spreading network of fibers. Small projections called root hairs grow along the length of the root and soak up water. Xerophytes produce more root hairs the drier it is. Tall, columnar cacti often have long, thick tap roots that grow deep into the ground to act as anchors. They also have a network of fibrous surface roots to soak up all available water. Many cacti have thick, turniplike roots, often larger than the stem, which store water and food.

Small tops, large roots

Bean capers (*Zygophyllum* species; see below) are found in Australia, Africa, the Middle East, and the Canary Islands. The succulent leaves and stems usually grow very slowly and a plant just 27 inches tall may be over 100 years old. The fibrous network of roots is enormous.

A single square yard of plant above ground will have almost 18 square yards of roots below ground. This vast network of roots explains why many desert plants are widely spaced.

Water and Food Transportation

Water is carried from the roots to all parts of the plant in the xylem vessels. During transpiration, water evaporates from the surface of the leaf or stem and pulls more water up the xylem from the roots as it does so. Food is carried in the phloem from the leaves or stem, where it is made, to the root, where it may be stored.

phloem

food

xylem

root hairs

water and minerals

Water stores

Many succulents have a thickened, swollen root or caudex. For example, *Echinocereus poselgeri*, the dahlia cactus, is a relatively small, slender, scrambling plant with large dahlia-like tubers. *Peniocereus*, the deerhorn cactus, has slender, straggling, twiggy stems with beautiful flowers. Its water-filled tubers can weigh up to 40 pounds. The stem of *Neoporteria wagenknechtii*, a globular cactus, has tubercles and is very spiny. The swollen root is much larger than the stem.

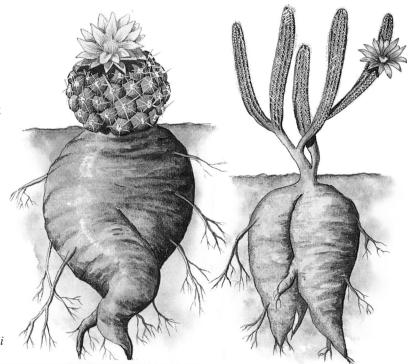

Neoporteria wagenknechtii

Echinocereus poselgeri,
the dahlia cactus

A swollen caudex

Many succulents, such as *Ipomoea*, a member of the convolvulus family, have a large swollen caudex. They usually have short stems, grasslike leaves, and large flowers. Many euphorbias, such as *E. rubella*, *E. fusca* and *E. bupleurifolia* (see left), have a large conelike caudex. The branches and leaves usually form a dense rosette.

25

NEW PLANTS FROM OLD

Like all living things, plants must make new plants in order for the group to survive. In many plants this can be done in two ways: sexually by producing flowers that bear male and female cells (see p. 28), and asexually by pieces of the parent plant breaking off and growing into new plants. This second type of reproduction is called **vegetative reproduction**. The main disadvantage with this is that all the offspring are exactly the same as the parent plant. There is no mixing of the characteristics of the parent plants and so no variation to allow them to adapt to changing conditions.

The main advantage is that the seedling stage, which is when most young plants die, is eliminated.

The young plants form in a variety of ways. Opuntias can grow roots or shoots from most parts of their body. If their prickly, detachable joints get broken off during a storm or by passing animals, they quickly develop roots and grow into new plants. They can multiply in this way at a very fast rate and spread rapidly over a large area. Other succulents develop small plants from the base of the stem. In others, the fleshy leaves can form roots and grow into independent plants.

Growing new plants
Some bryophyllums develop small plants around the edges or at the tips of their leaves. One species, *Bryophyllum tubiflorum* (shown right), produces young plants on short stalks near the tip of the cylindrical leaves. These baby plants have rounded leaves that form a cup shape. If a water drop strikes this cup and depresses it, the stalk acts like a catapult, flinging the small plantlet up to 5 feet away.

Leaf or plant?

Many leaf succulents like *Sedum* and *Calandrinia* produce new plants from single fleshy leaves. Sedums often produce their leaves on a long, trailing stem. These leaves can take root if detached from the plant during a storm or by animals. Similarly *Calandrinia*, found in Australia and South America, has a central rosette of succulent leaves from which long stems radiate. The stems support fleshy leaves that often take root as they straggle across the desert sands.

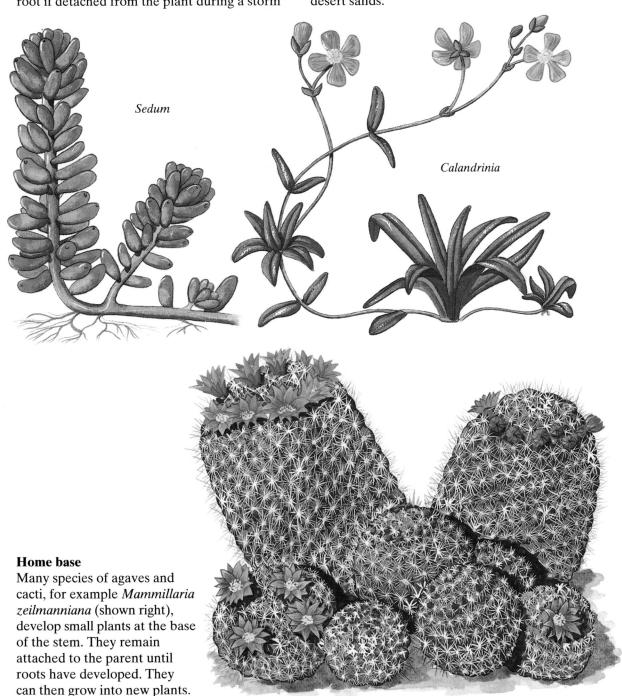

Sedum

Calandrinia

Home base

Many species of agaves and cacti, for example *Mammillaria zeilmanniana* (shown right), develop small plants at the base of the stem. They remain attached to the parent until roots have developed. They can then grow into new plants.

BRILLIANT FLOWERS

Many succulents produce brilliantly colored, often highly scented, flowers. These flowers are not just objects of beauty, they are essential for **sexual reproduction**. Their color, smell, and shape have one function: to attract **pollinators** such as insects and birds.

Although they may look very different, all flowers have the same basic structure. The flower buds are usually protected by special leaves called **sepals**. Beneath these lie the **petals**, which protect the male and female parts of the flower and attract the pollinators. The male part, the **stamen**, is made up of an **anther**, which produces the pollen (male cells), and a stalk or **filament**. The female part is a **carpel**. Pollination occurs when pollen is transferred to the female **stigma**. The male cell grows down the **style** to the **ovary**. The male cell **fertilizes** or joins with the female cell, the **ovule**, to form a **seed**.

Under suitable conditions, the seed will **germinate** and grow into a new plant. Unlike vegetative reproduction, the plants formed are not identical to the parent plants. This means that they may be able to survive in different places.

Daytime blooms
Many cacti and succulents bloom during the day. They are usually brilliantly colored and attract insects such as flies and bees, and sometimes hummingbirds. Many produce large amounts of nectar, a sugary liquid on which the visitors feed. Some are trumpet-shaped and are usually pollinated by bees or birds. Others are star-shaped with a different-colored center that leads the insect down into the flower. Some flowers are enormous, up to 15 inches across; others, like those of *Melocactus*, usually measure less than an inch.

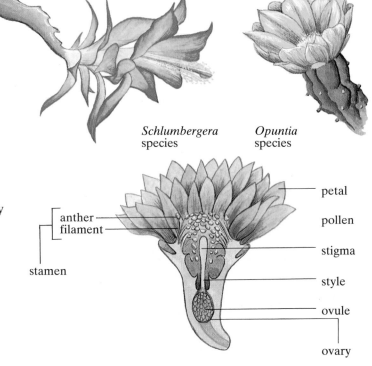

Schlumbergera species

Opuntia species

anther
filament
stamen

petal
pollen
stigma
style
ovule
ovary

White for night

Night-blooming succulents usually have pale, strongly scented flowers that are pollinated by moths or bats. Bat-pollinated flowers are usually easy to reach and produce a great deal of pollen and lots of sticky nectar. Some are bell-shaped and the bats have to force their way past pollen-laden anthers to reach the nectar. The night-blooming *Cereus* cactus (see right) is visited by the hawk moth, and the giant saguaro by the long-nosed bat.

Carrion flowers

African carrion flowers like *Stapelia gettleffii* (see left) have large orange- or brown-mottled flowers up to 15 inches across. Their foul smell and appearance attracts pollinating flies, who are so fooled by the plant's resemblance to rotting meat that they often lay eggs on the flowers. Some flowers are covered in hairs that look like mold, making the disguise even more effective.

29

FRUITS AND SEEDS

After a succulent has flowered, the petals wither and die. The fertilized ovules develop into seeds and the ovary swells around the seeds to form a protective **fruit**. Many fruits are long-lasting, juicy, and edible. Some fruits are tiny; others reach the size of small oranges or larger. They may be fleshy like *Opuntia* "berries," or dry like the complex seed cases of mesembryanthemums.

The seeds are carried away from the parent plant in various ways. Many rodents and birds eat the fleshy fruits of succulents. The seeds pass through the animal's gut unharmed and are excreted (passed out) in the droppings. The seeds of dry fruits are released when the seed case dries and splits. They are carried away by insects, blown away by the wind, or swept away in a stream of water when it rains.

The seed contains the young plant which, under certain conditions, will start to grow. Many require a heavy rainfall; a heavy dewfall will not trigger **germination**. The seed coat, or testa, of many succulents contains a chemical that prevents growth. Only when this is washed away by rain will the seed germinate and grow into a new plant.

Seed cases
African mesembryanthemums produce very beautiful and complex seed cases (see right). They remain tightly closed during dry weather but open if they get wet. The inside of the capsule forms a star shape and the seeds inside are often washed away by raindrops splashing into the opening.

Floating seeds

The seeds of some succulents are dispersed as rainwater washes over the surface of the soil. This is particularly important in desert regions where torrential rain causes temporary rivers and floods. The seeds of some *Lithops* and *Conophytum* (fruits containing seeds are shown on the right) have developed a small air pocket in their seed coat. This enables them to float for several days, ensuring that they are spread over a wide area. Seeds of some cacti, such as *Frailea* species, are also buoyant.

A time to grow

Seeds will only germinate after a certain time and under certain conditions. For a seed to grow it needs water, oxygen, and the right temperature. In hot deserts, like this one in Mexico (see left), cacti seeds germinate best between 85°F and 105°F. Most succulent seeds germinate and develop a rooting system very rapidly. This ensures that the new plant is established before the moisture dries up.

FOOD FOR ALL

As with all plants, succulents are an important source of food for the animals living alongside them. They form the primary link in the food chains of arid **ecosystems**. Many insects, birds, and mammals depend on the flowers, fruit, and leaves of succulent plants for both food and water. Some desert animals never drink; they obtain all their water from the plants they eat.

Beetles and small mammals such as rodents feed on the flowers as well as the fruits and seeds of succulents. Others use plants to provide shade and shelter, away from the scorching heat of the midday sun or the freezing cold nights. Insects such as grasshoppers and locusts migrate to desert regions when the succulents are in bloom. Many of them lay their eggs at the beginning of the "wet" season so that the developing nymphs (young insects) can feed on the flowers of the cacti and succulents. The insects themselves are preyed on by birds, lizards, and rodents. These in turn are hunted by larger rodents and the fennec fox. Without the drought-resistant succulents, life in these arid regions could not survive.

Desert life

In arid and semiarid desert regions of Africa (see below), succulents form an important part of the food chain. The juicy stems, buds, and flowers of carallumas and aloes are eaten by hungry grasshoppers and their nymphs. These in turn are eaten by birds and by tiny desert gerbils.

The saguaro community

The giant saguaro, like most cacti, has a vertically ribbed stem. Its surface is covered with rows of spines. These do not, however, prevent many desert animals from burrowing into its trunk or eating its fruits and flowers (see right). The flowers and fruits provide food and drink for many birds, including woodpeckers and finches.

The Galia woodpecker hollows a nest cavity out of the pulpy stem. The fledglings feed on the many insects attracted by the saguaro's flowers and fruit. After the young woodpeckers have left, other birds like elf owls take over their nest. The elf owl is so dependent on these nesting sites that it is only found where both saguaros and woodpeckers exist.

The Flower Feeders

The flowers of succulents are a source of food for many animals (see below).

Butterflies often drink nectar from the small star-shaped flowers of sedums.

Many insect nymphs feed on the stamens and anthers of cactus flowers.

The sunbirds of Africa feed on nectar. They have long, slender beaks, specially adapted for reaching deep into the tubular flowers of African aloes.

SURVIVAL MECHANISMS

The grazing animals that feed on succulents range from tiny sap-sucking insects to those that nibble their way through leaves, flowers, and berries. Larger mammals feed on the entire plant. As succulent plants are usually slow-growing, it takes them a long time to recover from being grazed. Plants cannot escape from their enemies, so they have developed special armor and weapons to protect themselves.

Cacti, for example, have developed spines and prickles as an effective defense (see p. 22). Many euphorbias are not only often spiny, they also produce an unpleasant milky sap or latex. In other succulents, a mat of fine hairs keeps small insects from reaching the juicy tissues beneath. Yuccas and agaves produce very stiff rosettes of leaves that often have sharp, serrated edges and a thick, almost inedible, cuticle.

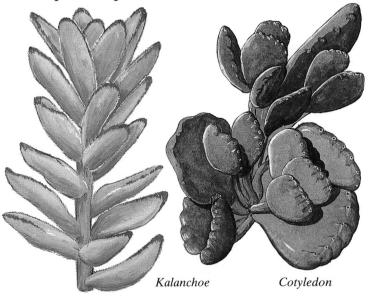

Kalanchoe   *Cotyledon*   *Fenestraria*

Surviving the sun

Too much sun can damage a plant. It not only dries the plant out, but the ultraviolet rays and heat can damage its tissues. Many succulents' leaves have overcome this problem by having a protective layer to deflect or disperse the heat. This may be a layer of hairs (*Kalanchoe*, above left), a felty covering, a white or silvery surface, or a thickened, waxy skin with a tubercled (lumpy) surface (*Cotyledon* species, above center).

Many mesembryanthemums have special protective mechanisms. For example, the fleshy-leaved window plant, *Fenestraria aurantiaca* (shown above right), lies buried beneath the sand with only the flattened top of its leaves exposed. The upper surface contains a "window" made of a layer of crystals. This limits the effect of the sun's rays on the sensitive tissues below, but allows enough light through to reach the chlorophyll layer deep within the leaf.

34

A different approach to ensuring survival can be seen in seeds that release chemicals that prevent other seeds from germinating. Similarly, the roots of some desert plants produce chemicals that inhibit the growth of other plants. This may explain why some succulents are so widely spaced in deserts and semideserts.

Only stones?
Stone mimics (*Lithops*, see above) grow in rocky wastes. Their mottled gray or brown rounded leaves resemble the pebbles or stones that surround them. There are over 50 different kinds of these pebble plants which come in a variety of shades and colors. Only the tops of their flattened surfaces protrude above the ground. Their camouflage is almost perfect.

Uneven partners
Many plants use others to guarantee their survival, either as support or as shade from the sun. For example, seedlings of the giant saguaro will germinate more readily in the shade of the *Palo verde* tree (see below). The rooting system of the saguaro is very effective and eventually the cactus absorbs so much water that the tree dies. The dahlia cactus, on the other hand, rarely reaches 2 inches unless it is physically supported by other plants.

A CHANGING WORLD

The Earth has changed greatly since its formation some 4.5 billion years ago. During its long history, periods of heat and cold have altered the climate, and land and sea masses have changed their shape and position. However, with a few exceptions, these natural changes happened so slowly that plants and animals could adapt to them. In recent times, changes brought about by people have happened rapidly and animals and plants have suffered.

Many habitats have been lost. There are two main causes: trees are chopped down, and grasslands are plowed up to provide land for buildings and farming. Less fertile grasslands are often used to graze domestic animals like cattle and goats. The leaves of trees, shrubs, and grasses are nibbled away. Eventually even tough plants such as aloes may disappear.

Meager grasslands are often dug up to grow crops. The natural vegetation is lost and the soil is not fertile enough to support crops for more than a few years. Eventually the fields turn to sandy wastes.

Too many animals
In many arid and semiarid regions, overgrazing by domestic animals, especially goats, has had a disastrous effect on grasslands (see above). Once the grass is removed from savanna or semidesert regions, there is nothing to bind the topsoil, which is blown or washed away by sudden rainstorms. Usually grass cannot regrow in these areas, but thorn bushes and cacti often become established.

Watering the desert

Many desert and semidesert regions are being reclaimed and used to grow crops. In some places artesian wells are sunk to provide much needed water to **irrigate** the land. In others, dams are built and water is pumped through vast pipes to the arid fields, as here in Arizona (see below). However, irrigation itself can lead to problems.

As there are no trees or dense vegetation to protect the soil from the heat of the sun, the water evaporates very quickly, leaving behind the salts that were dissolved in it. Most plants cannot grow in salty soils, and so one problem has been replaced by another. People are learning from the mistakes of the past and are now more careful when setting up irrigation programs.

Disappearing rain forests

The tropical rain forests of Central and South America, home to many beautiful and unusual epiphytic cacti, are being destroyed at the rate of about 25 acres a minute. When a tree falls, all the life that is living on it also dies.

The biggest problem that these cacti face, growing high up in the trees, is getting enough water and sometimes enough light. Their thick, waxy cuticle cuts down water loss and their flattened stems give a larger surface to soak up sunlight. As there are few animals to graze on them, their protective spines are reduced to fine hairs or lost altogether. Some, like *Rhipsalis* and *Schlumbergera*, form cascades of branching stems (see right). Others like *Hatiora* have long twiglike stems. As the forests disappear, so do thousands of unusual and rare plants.

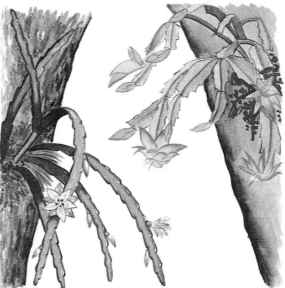

37

THE INVADERS

Many succulents have been introduced into other parts of the world as garden plants, crops, or in the case of cacti, as hedges. Their ability to survive in harsh conditions and to spread by vegetative reproduction (see p. 26) can cause them to become weeds, growing out of control.

For example, the prickly pear, *Opuntia*, was introduced into Australia in the 1880s – 1890s as a garden curiosity and for use as fencing and feed for domestic cattle. It soon became a serious pest, invading both farmland and scrub.

Opuntia and many other similar cacti have also spread into dry areas of the Mediterranean. When introduced into arid regions of North Africa, cacti reproduce very rapidly, often choking out the natural vegetation.

A prickly problem
In the late 1800s, prickly pears were introduced as hedging into Australia (see below). By 1900 they had spread over 10 million acres and by 1925 they covered more than 60 million acres. The Argentinian moth *Cactoblastis cactorum* was introduced and by 1938 the caterpillars had attacked and destroyed 25 million acres of prickly pear, restoring the land for farming. Such methods of biological control are not always so successful!

Island invasions

The natural vegetation of many islands, especially in tropical and subtropical regions, is under threat from introduced succulents. Often the natural vegetation on these islands has already been partly destroyed by the introduction of herds of domesticated goats. This allows the "foreign" plants to become established more easily.

Some of the Galapagos Islands, for example, are being overtaken by yuccas to the detriment of the unique original flora. The Galapagos Islands are the only place in the world where prickly pears reach the size of trees (see right). They may have developed in this way to protect their juicy pads from the local giant tortoises which graze on plants.

The ornamentals

Succulents are grown throughout the world as unusual ornamental plants for the home and garden. Many agaves, yuccas, and cacti can be seen growing in Mediterranean countries and some will even grow in much cooler regions of Europe, such as southern Britain. For example, *Aeonium arboreum* (see below), a member of the crassula family originally from North Africa and the Canary Islands, is often found in more northerly Mediterranean countries where it grows well and has become naturalized.

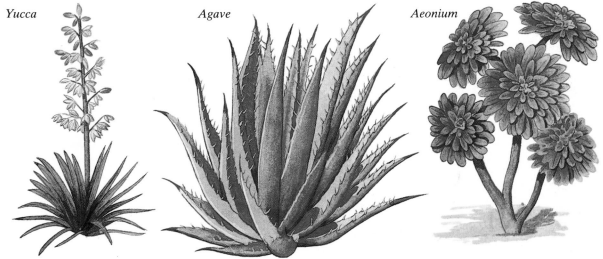

Yucca   *Agave*   *Aeonium*

THE COLLECTORS

Many of the exotic plants popular in homes and gardens throughout the world arose elsewhere. Plants have been collected for centuries. Even the ancient Egyptians collected plants. In the 1800s and 1900s collecting became a very important part of plant research. Some collectors in the 1800s destroyed hundreds of plants when gathering rare specimens. They dug them up without thought for the long-term effect on the natural habitat or whether the plants could survive in their new homes.

Today, although large-scale collecting of plants still continues, many countries protect their rare species. There are also many societies that try to protect rare plants. The Convention on International Trade in Endangered Species of Wild Fauna and Flora (CITES) and the World Wide Fund for Nature (WWF) both help to preserve endangered plants and habitats. However, as some people will pay a great deal of money to own a rare specimen, poachers are even willing to risk taking plants from national parks.

Saved!
Conservation, the protection of plants and animals in their natural environment, is now becoming very important. This has taken several forms, from the re-creation of special habitats from wasteland to the formation of national parks (see the Saguaro National Monument, Arizona, right) and nature reserves that protect as many threatened species as possible. Many species that are extinct in the wild are preserved by cultivation in special botanical gardens. This is valuable in many ways: it prevents final extinction and gives the opportunity for re-establishing the plant in its natural habitat.

Famous names

There have been many famous plant collectors. The plants they discovered are often named after them. For example, in the early 1800s, the American explorers Lewis and Clark (see right) discovered and named many new plants when they ventured into the interior of North America. William and Joseph Hooker also collected many rare specimens, most of which were taken back to England to be studied at the Royal Botanic Gardens, Kew.

Endangered succulents

Throughout the world, flowering plants are under threat from over-collection, and cacti and other succulents are no exception (see below). As these plants are very slow growing, it takes a long time to replace them in their natural habitat. Large spectacular cacti or rare specimens are highly prized by collectors and many have been dug up. For example, several species from Mexico and the southern U.S. are close to extinction (dying out), as are unusual succulents from Africa and Australia. Even common cacti are dug up by the hundreds for sale to the trade.

Luckhoffia beukmannii is very rare in its native habitat, Cape Province in South Africa.

Strombocactus disciformis is a highly prized cactus. In the 1980s, one plant is said to have sold for over $300.

USES AND CULTIVATION

In the past, cacti and other succulents were used to make many useful products. Opuntias in particular were important. In Mexico, cochineal (a red food coloring) was once made from cochineal insects that were bred on opuntias. Most of it is now made from aniline dyes, but some natural cochineal is still produced and it is now becoming cheaper to make.

In many parts of Central and South America, opuntias are still important. The young shoots, flowers, and buds are eaten as vegetables. The large succulent fruits of some *Cereus* and *Opuntia* are also eaten. They ripen in the dry season and so can be very important if other crops fail.

When giant cacti like the saguaro get old, the stems become woody and tough. Although light, this "wood" is strong and can be used to build houses or make household goods. It is also used as fuel in areas where trees are few and far between.

Many succulents are grown as hedging. Poisonous African spurges are used by hill villagers in northern Nigeria to protect their villages from attack and as pens for their animals. *Pachycereus marginatus* and spiny opuntias are used to provide thick cattle-proof hedging in South America.

Desert fruits

Some opuntias are grown commercially, particularly in Mexico and southern Europe (Sicily), where they are known as Indian fig, tuna, or prickly pear. They can be eaten fresh or dried or can be cooked in various ways. They can even be fermented into an alcoholic drink called coloncha. Prickly pear or Indian figs, are now being exported to many temperate countries. Another cactus fruit, the "pitahaya amarilla" (*Selenicereus megalanthus*), is now imported from Colombia and sold in many supermarkets.

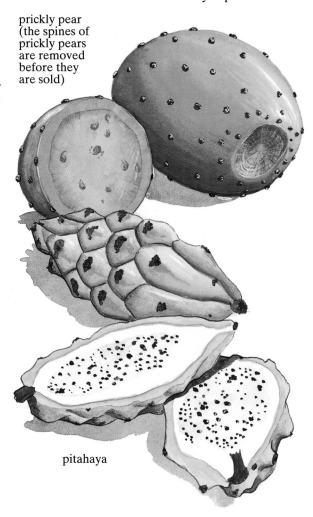

prickly pear (the spines of prickly pears are removed before they are sold)

pitahaya

Ancient medicines

Many cacti and succulents are important medicines. The stem pads of many opuntias are used as "bandages" to relieve swelling and bruising. A juice made from queen of the night (*Selenicereus grandiflorus*) contains a chemical that is useful in treating heart disease. The sap of *Aloe vera* is used to prepare a soothing, green oil for sunburn and sore, dry skins. The mescal cactus or peyote (*Lophophora williamsii*, see right) contains several substances, including mescalin, that cause color and sound hallucinations (images that are not real). It formed an important part of the religious ceremonies of certain Mexican Indian tribes. An alcoholic Mexican drink called mescal, which has no such effect, is made from *Agave tequilana*.

Cultivating succulents

Succulents are very popular houseplants and many people grow them as a hobby. They are cultivated on a large commercial scale in many regions and can be bought at supermarkets and garden centers. Many new varieties are formed by fertilizing one type with another and growing new plants from the resulting seeds. Most cacti are grown from cuttings or from tiny new plants produced as offshoots. Thousands are sold worldwide and they form an important part of the horticultural (garden) industry.

GLOSSARY

ANGIOSPERM – Plants with flowers and seeds that grow into fruit.

ANTHER – The part of the male stamen in which pollen grains are made.

AREOLE – Cushionlike growing points from which the spines of cacti grow.

CARPEL – The female part of a flower, made up of an ovary, style, and stigma.

CAUDEX – A swollen, fleshy root or stem base.

CHLOROPHYLL – The green pigment in plants that traps the energy of the sun which is used in photosynthesis.

COLONIZE – The growth and settlement of plants in a new area.

CUTICLE – The waterproof, waxy skin of leaves and stems.

DICOTYLEDON – Plants that produce two seed-leaves or cotyledons.

ECOSYSTEM – A community of plants and animals living together and depending on one another for survival.

EPIPHYTE – A plant that grows in the air supported by another plant.

EVOLVE – The gradual change over a long time of animal and plant groups. This may result in new groups of plants or animals developing.

FERTILIZE – When a male pollen cell joins with a female ovule.

FILAMENT – The stalk of the male stamen.

FRUIT – The part of a flower that contains and protects the developing seed or seeds.

GERMINATE – The sprouting of a seed to give a new plant.

GERMINATION – When a seed begins to grow.

GYMNOSPERM – Nonflowering plants that have seeds contained in woody cones or fleshy scales.

HABITAT – The place where a plant or animal lives.

IRRIGATE – To supply dry land with water by means of canals, ditches, or sprinkler systems.

MONOCOTYLEDON – Plants that have only one seed-leaf or cotyledon.

OVARY – The part of a flower containing the ovule.

OVULE – The female cell in a plant that, after being fertilized by a male cell, becomes a seed.

PETALS – Parts of the flower that surround the stamens and carpels.

PHLOEM – Plant tissue that carries food.

PHOTOSYNTHESIS – The process by which green plants make sugar from carbon dioxide gas and water using the energy in sunlight.

POLLINATOR – An insect or animal that transfers pollen from one plant to another.

RESPIRATION – A process in which oxygen is taken in from the air and used to break down food. Energy and carbon dioxide are released.

SAP – The liquid, made up of water and nutrients, that circulates in a plant.

SEED – A fully developed, fertilized ovule. It contains an embryo (young plant) and a food store, and can grow into a new plant.

SEPALS – The parts of a plant that form a ring below the petals. They often protect the young bud.

SEXUAL REPRODUCTION – The fusing of a male sex cell with a female sex cell to form a new plant.

STAMEN – The male part of a flower.

STIGMA – The tip of the style which receives the pollen.

STOMATA (singular stoma) – The pores on the surface of a leaf through which gases move.

STYLE – A stem joining the stigma to the ovary.

TRANSPIRATION – The flow of water from the root of a plant up the stem into the leaves and out into the air.

TUBERCLES – Swellings or growths of the cuticle of the stems or leaves of succulent plants.

VEGETATIVE REPRODUCTION – The growth of a new plant from a part of the parent plant other than the seeds.

XEROPHYTE – Plants that can live for long periods without water.

XYLEM – Plant tissue that carries water from the roots to other parts of the plant.

FURTHER READING

For children

Cactus by Cynthia Overbeck; Lerner, 1982.

Cactus: The All-American Plant by Anita Holmes; Four Winds, 1982.

For adults

The Cacti of the United States & Canada by Lyman Benson; Stanford Univ. Press, 1982.

Encyclopedia of Cacti by Willy Culman, et. al.; Timber Press, 1987.

SUCCULENTS IN THIS BOOK

Cacti
Cephalocereus senilis
Cereus species (*C.chalybaeus*; *C. spegazzinii*)
Deerhorn cactus (*Peniocereus* species)
Dudleya species (*D. farinosa*)
Echinocactus platyacanthus
Echinocereus species (*E. viridiflorus*; dahlia
    cactus, *E. poselgeri*)
Escobaria species (*E. vivipara*)
Ferocactus species (*F. emoryi*; *F. latispinus*)
Frailea species
Giant saguaro (*Carnegiea gigantea*)
Gymnocalycium castellanosii
Hatiora species
Maihuenia species (*M. poeppigii*)
Mammillaria species (*M. hahniana*; *M. senilis*;
    M. zeilmanniana)
Melocactus species
Neoporteria wagenknechtii
Opuntia species
Pachycereus species (*P. pringlei*; *P. marginatus*)
Pereskia species
Peyote or mescal (*Lophophora williamsii*)
Rhipsalis species (*R. russellii*; *R. baccifera*)
Schlumbergera species
Selenicereus species (pitahaya, *S. megalanthus*;
    queen of the night, *S. grandiflorus*)
Strombocactus disciformis
Turbinicarpus valdezianus

Other succulents
Aeonium species (*A. arboreum*)
Agaves (*Agave* species; *A americana*;
    A. tequilana)
Aichryson species (*A. dichotomum*)
Aloes (*Aloe* species; *A. arborescens*;
    A. humilis; *A. vera*)
Ant plants (*Myrmecodia* species; *Hydnophytum*
    species)
Baobab or elephant trees (*Adansonia digitata*;
    Brachychiton species)
Bean capers (*Zygophyllum* species)
Bryophyllums (*Bryophyllum* species;
    B. tubiflorum)

Calandrinia species (*C. polyandra*)
Caralluma species (*C. europaea*; *C. foetida*)
Ceropegia species (*C. dichotoma*)
Cotyledon undulata
Crassulas (*Crassula* species; *C. barbata*)
Dischidia species (*D. rafflesiana*)
Echeverias (*Echeveria* species; *E. agavoides*)
Euphorbias (*Euphorbia* species; *E. bupleurifolia*;
    E. fusca; *E. grandicornis*; *E. rubella*)
Greenovia species
Hoyas (*Hoya* species; *H. carnosa*)
Ipomoea species
Kalanchoe species (*K. tomentosa*)
Lewisia species (bitterroot, *L. rediviva*)
Luckhoffia beukmannii
Mesembryanthemums (*Carpobrotus* species;
    Conophytum species; *Faucaria* species;
    Fenestraria aurantiaca; *Lithops* species;
    Nananthus species; *Ruschia* species)
Meterostachys species
Orostachys species (*O. japonicus*)
Pachypodium species (*P. geayi*)
Portulaca species (*P.decipiens*)
Rhodiola species
Sedums (*Sedum* species; *S. dasyphyllum*;
    S. spectabile)
Sempervivum species (*S. arachnoideum*;
    S. montanum)
Senecio haworthii
Sinocrassula species
Stapelia species (*S. gigantea*)
Trichocaulon species (*T. cactiforme*)
Welwitschia species
Yucca species

INDEX